THE GIVER
NOTES

including
- *Life and Background of the Author*
- *Introduction to the Novel*
- *A Brief Synopsis*
- *List of Characters*
- *Critical Commentaries*
- *Map of Jonas' Community in* The Giver
- *Critical Essays*
    Lowry's Major Themes
    Lowry's Style and Language
    What are Utopias and Dystopias?
    A Note About Infanticide and Euthanasia
- *Review Questions and Essay Topics*
- *Selected Bibliography*

by
Suzanne Pavlos, M.Ed.
Stephen F. Austin State University

INCORPORATED

LINCOLN, NEBRASKA 68501

OUACHITA TECHNICAL COLLEGE

Editor

Gary Carey, M.A.
University of Colorado

Consulting Editor

James L. Roberts, Ph.D.
Department of English
University of Nebraska

ISBN 0-7645-8510-X
© Copyright 1999
by
Cliffs Notes, Inc.
All Rights Reserved
Printed in U.S.A.

1999 Printing

The Cliffs Notes logo, the names "Cliffs" and Cliffs Notes," and the black and yellow diagonal-stripe cover design are all registered trademarks belonging to Cliffs Notes, Inc., and may not be used in whole or in part without written permission.

Cliffs Notes, Inc.   Lincoln, Nebraska

PZ
7
.L9673
C638g
1999

CONTENTS

Centerspread: Map of Jonas' Community in *The Giver*

THE GIVER
Notes

LIFE AND BACKGROUND OF THE AUTHOR

Lois Lowry's first book, *A Summer to Die*, was published in 1977. Since then, she has written over twenty novels for young adults and has won numerous awards, including two prestigious Newbery awards, one for *Number the Stars* and the other for *The Giver*. Lowry doesn't rely on awards to determine her success as a writer but, rather, on how well she communicates with her readers about individuality, life, and relationships. Her books portray sensitive, intelligent, witty protagonists who are faced with challenges and choices in life. She writes about topics that range from the humorous escapades of Anastasia Krupnik to Jonas' serious realization in *The Giver* that he has been living his life like a robot.

Lowry was born on March 20, 1937, in Honolulu, Hawaii, to Robert E. Hammersberg, a United States Army dentist, and Katherine Landis Hammersberg. Because her father was a career army officer, Lowry often moved during her childhood. From Hawaii, her family relocated to New York, and during World War II, she, her mother, and her older sister, Helen, lived with her mother's family in Pennsylvania while her father was stationed overseas. During this time in Pennsylvania, Lowry's grandfather showered her with attention and affection, but her step-grandmother merely tolerated her. Because Lowry was a shy, introverted child, she sought companionship and entertainment in the wonderful worlds that existed within the books she found in her grandfather's library. After the war, Lowry and her family joined her father in Tokyo, Japan, where they lived for two years in an Americanized community.

At the outbreak of the Korean War in 1950, Lowry returned to the United States to attend a small, private high school in New York City. She graduated from high school in a class of close to fifty students. The caption under her senior picture in the school yearbook reads, "Future Novelist." The following fall, Lowry entered Pembroke College, a branch of Brown University, in Rhode Island, to pursue her childhood dream of becoming a writer. She completed her sophomore year of college, and then, at the age of nineteen, she did what so many other women did during the 1950s: She set her studies aside to get married. Because her husband, Donald Lowry, was a naval officer, Lowry resumed a military lifestyle that included traveling and living wherever her husband was stationed. She and her husband lived in California, Connecticut, Florida, and South Carolina, and when her husband left the service to attend Harvard Law School, they moved to Cambridge, Massachusetts. After her husband finished law school, the Lowry family, which now included four children, settled in Portland, Maine. Lowry eventually received a bachelor's degree in 1972 from the University of Southern Maine and then immediately began work on a master's degree.

While attending graduate school, Lowry established herself as an accomplished freelance journalist. She began writing stories and articles that appeared in publications such as *Redbook*, *Yankee*, and *Down East*, as well as in newspapers. She also edited two textbooks—*Black American Literature* (1973) and *Literature of the American Revolution* (1974), both written by J. Weston Walsh—and became a photographer, specializing in photographs of children. In 1978, a collection of her photographs of buildings and houses was published in a book titled *Here at Kennebunkport*.

Lowry's first novel, *A Summer to Die* (1977), is about the relationship between two adolescent sisters, Meg and Molly, and the effect that Molly's death, as a result of leukemia, has on the family. Lowry based the relationship between Meg and Molly on her own memories of her relationship with her older sister, Helen, as they were growing up, and on the feelings and emotions that she felt when Helen died of cancer. Lowry experienced other heartaches, as well. Grey, her oldest son and a fighter pilot in the United States Air Force, was killed in a plane crash. In addition, Lowry has a daughter who became disabled as a result of a disease involving the central nervous system. Her daughter's disability has reinforced Lowry's belief that people are "connected" despite their physical differences.

In 1977, Lowry and her husband divorced, and Lowry remained in Maine for the next two years, continuing to write. After completing another serious novel, *Find a Stranger, Say Goodbye* (1978), Lowry moved to Boston. Because she had been writing about serious and sad issues, she decided to write a humorous short story about a ten-year-old girl named Anastasia Krupnik. Anastasia is a gangly girl who wears glasses, has messy blonde hair, and is always getting into mischief. Lowry liked Anastasia and her family so much that the short story became the first chapter of her novel *Anastasia Krupnik* (1979), the first in a series of novels about Anastasia.

Lowry divides her time between her house in Cambridge, Massachusetts, and her nineteenth-century farmhouse in New Hampshire. When she isn't at her desk writing, she likes to garden, cook, and knit. She enjoys reading memoirs and biographies, taking exotic, adventurous trips, and going to as many movies as possible. She writes for about five hours each day, working on more than one project at a time. Although her novels cover a variety of topics and range in tone from serious to humorous, they share many of the same themes: individuality, freedom, and the importance of memory. Through her writing, Lowry communicates the message that people must be aware that everything they do affects other people, the environment, and the world.

INTRODUCTION TO THE NOVEL

As Lois Lowry stated in her acceptance speech when she won the Newbery Medal for *The Giver*, she began writing a book that takes place in a utopia, where everything is perfect. She learned from her memories that living in a perfect society is not risk-free, that dangers lurk in a society in which everything is the same and in which the freedom to choose how to live has been given up. Lowry's memories are the basis for *The Giver*, and her writing conveys lessons about life to her readers.

Lowry lived with her family in an Americanized community in Tokyo, Japan, when she was a young girl. The community was very familiar and safe because it resembled other communities in the United States, where she'd lived earlier in her life. While in Tokyo, Lowry oftentimes rode her bike to visit a nearby Japanese community, where everything was foreign to her, including the language, colors, smells, and even the way people dressed and acted. Lowry used this experience to create the community in which Jonas, the protagonist, or main character, in *The Giver*, lives. Jonas' community is very predictable, familiar, and safe. Lowry also created Elsewhere, the world outside the community that is believed to be different, dangerous, and inferior.

Years after Lowry interviewed and photographed an artist named Carl Nelson (whose photograph is on the cover of the Laurel-Leaf edition of *The Giver*), she learned that Nelson had become blind. Because Nelson was a painter, Lowry wondered what it must have been like for Nelson when his world became colorless. Lowry used this situation to create a colorless community in *The Giver*, where people do not see color; therefore, everything has the same color—*none*.

Lowry remembered other events that reinforced her belief that memory is necessary and important if we are to live meaningful, well-rounded lives. One event involved her parents, who lived together in the same nursing home when they were older. Lowry's father was in good shape physically, but he had lost most of his memory. Lowry's mother was dying, but she was able to share all of her memories with Lowry. The irony of the situation—a father in good shape physically but without any memory, and a mother in poor health physically but mentally alert—prompted Lowry to realize how important it is to remember and share memories with others. Another event that helped shape *The Giver* was when a woman, referring to Lowry's book *Number the Stars*, asked Lowry why incidents relating to the Holocaust have to be told over and over again. Lowry's German-born daughter-in-law told Lowry that such stories have to be repeated so that no one will forget the horror of what happened and allow it to happen again. In *The Giver*, Jonas understands that memories are necessary so that people can learn from the past and lead happier, more fulfilling lives.

Lowry also remembered a time when she and other girls whom she was living with during college completely ignored another girl because the girl was different. When people are perceived as being different in *The Giver*, they are "released"—in the novel, meaning killed—from the community. Lowry's own memories emphasize the themes in *The Giver*, including the importance of individuality and freedom of choice, and the need for caring relationships between all human beings despite their differences.

A BRIEF SYNOPSIS

Lowry narrates *The Giver* in third person ("He said," as opposed to "I said," which is called first person), using a limited omniscient viewpoint (only Jonas' thoughts and feelings are revealed). Through Jonas' eyes, his community appears to be a utopia—a perfect place—that is self-contained and isolated from Elsewhere, every other place in the world. No evidence of disease, hunger, poverty, war, or lasting pain exists in the community. Jonas' family, like all other families in the community, includes a caring mother and father and two children—one male child and one female child. Jonas' mother has an important job with the Department of Justice, and his father has a job as a Nurturer, taking care of newborns. Jonas has one younger sister, Lily. His family *seems* ideal. Each morning, they discuss their dreams that they had the previous night; during the evening meal, they share feelings about the events of the day, comforting and supporting each other according to the rules of the community.

As we learn more about Jonas' family, we also learn about the community as a whole. Family units must apply for children, spouses do not get to choose one another but, instead, are matched, and grandparents do not exist. All of a sudden, this utopia that Lowry has created doesn't seem quite right. The mood is foreboding, a feeling that something bad will happen. This mood suggests that Jonas' community is far from perfect.

A long time ago, the people in Jonas' community chose to have the community ruled by a Committee of Elders. The Committee of Elders controls everyone and everything, blasting rules and reprimands from loudspeakers located throughout the community, including in every family dwelling. A total of fifty infants are born to Birthmothers every year. Each peer group is identified by its age—for example, Threes, Sevens, Nines—and must follow specific rules about appropriate clothing, haircuts, and activities for that particular peer group. When children become Eights, they begin mandatory volunteering and are closely observed by the Committee of Elders so that the committee can assign a lifelong profession to each child at the Ceremony of Twelve, which takes place every year during the December Ceremony.

The Giver begins with Jonas' apprehension about his Ceremony of Twelve, when he will be assigned his lifelong job. He can guess which jobs his friends, Fiona and Asher, will be assigned, but he has no idea what his own job Assignment will be. At the Ceremony, Jonas learns that he has been selected to become the next Receiver of Memory, the highest position in the community.

Jonas begins training under the present Receiver of Memory, an older man whom Jonas calls The Giver. The Giver lives alone in private rooms that are lined with shelves full of books. Jonas' training involves receiving, from The Giver, all of the emotions and memories of experiences that the people in the community chose to give up to attain Sameness and the illusion of social order. The first memory that Jonas receives from The Giver is a sled ride down a snow-covered hill. Jonas has never before experienced going downhill, cold weather, or snow. Eventually, through memories, The Giver teaches Jonas about color, love, war, and pain. Jonas begins to understand the hypocrisy that exists in his community—that is, the illusion that everything in the community is good when in fact it isn't. The people *appear* to love each other, but they don't really know what love feels like because their lives are a charade; their reactions have been trained. Jonas realizes that people have given up their freedoms to feel and think as individuals, choosing instead to be controlled by others.

One day, Jonas asks The Giver if he can watch a video of a release his father performed on an infant earlier that morning. He watches and is horrified when he realizes that a release is really forced death by lethal injection. Jonas discusses his feelings with The Giver, and they decide on a plan that will force the people to give up Sameness. However, before they can carry out their plan, Jonas learns that Gabriel, a two-year-old infant who has been staying with Jonas' family unit because Gabriel has trouble sleeping through the night, is going to be released—killed. To prevent Gabriel from being killed, Jonas takes Gabriel, whom he loves, and together they ride a bicycle out of the community to Elsewhere. By escaping the community, all of the memories that Jonas has received from The Giver will be transmitted back to the citizens in the community, forcing them to experience feelings and emotions and to remember their past.

Jonas travels for days and days with Gabriel, who is dying from starvation and the cold weather. Finally, they come to the top of a hill where there is snow and a sled. They get on the sled and ride downhill toward music and Christmas lights. What actually happens to Jonas and Gabriel? Do they die? Are they dreaming? Do they go to a house with lights and music? Do they end up back in their original community? Do the people in the community change? All of these questions are left unanswered at the end of the book. Lowry intentionally writes an ambiguous ending so that readers can decide for themselves what happens to Jonas and Gabriel at the end of *The Giver*.

LIST OF CHARACTERS

Jonas

The protagonist, or main character, in the novel. Jonas is a sensitive, polite, compassionate twelve-year-old boy. At the December Ceremony, he is selected to become the new Receiver of Memory, the most honored position in the community. Jonas is quite complacent, or non-caring, before he begins his training as the new Receiver, but after he gains wisdom from memories and realizes that people gave up their freedoms for Sameness, he becomes angry and frustrated. During his training, Jonas acquires very deep emotional feelings and learns about love. He becomes a close friend of The Giver and risks his own life to save the citizens in his community.

Mother

Jonas' mother is an intelligent, sympathetic, and understanding person. She holds a prominent position at the Department of Justice. One of her job responsibilities is to punish people for breaking the strictly enforced rules of the community.

Father

Jonas' father is a shy, quiet, considerate, caring man. He is a Nurturer, responsible for the physical and emotional needs of every newborn child during the first few months of life. He is also responsible for the release—killing—of infants who are deemed worthless because something either emotional or physical, or both, is wrong with them.

Lily

Jonas' younger sister. Lily becomes an Eight during the December Ceremony that takes place toward the beginning of the book. She is a typically impatient child with straightforward, fairly simple feelings. For example, she is not concerned that her hair ribbons are always untied, and Lowry describes her as overly talkative.

Gabriel (Gabe)

A newchild (infant) who begins spending nights with Jonas' family unit because he needs extra attention and care. Gabe is a sweet child but does not sleep through the night and is not gaining weight as fast as the other newchildren. He ends up sleeping in Jonas' room and is able to receive memories from Jonas.

The Giver

The Giver is the current Receiver of Memory and trains Jonas to become the next Receiver. Because he carries the burden of the memories of the world, he suffers from the pain contained within the memories. He is lonely because he can't share his work with citizens in the community, and he is cynical and frustrated at times because he knows that the people gave up too much when they chose Sameness. He loves Jonas and the people in the community.

Asher

Jonas' best friend. Asher is a cheerful, friendly boy who makes a game out of everything. At the Ceremony of Twelve, he is assigned to be Assistant Director of Recreation.

Fiona

One of Jonas' good friends. Fiona is a very pretty girl who is sensitive, intelligent, quiet, and polite. She is assigned to be a Caretaker of the Old.

Larissa

An elderly woman who lives in the House of the Old. Jonas bathes her when he volunteers at the House of the Old. While being bathed, she tells Jonas about two elderly people who have been released recently.

Chief Elder

The leader of the community.

Fritz

Fritz lives in the dwelling next door to Jonas'. He is an awkward child who is always getting into trouble. Fritz turns nine years old at the December Ceremony and receives his own bicycle, as all Nines do.

Caleb

The first Caleb died when he was four years old by falling into the river that runs near the community. During the December Ceremony, the couple who were given the first Caleb receive a replacement child, also named Caleb.

Rosemary

Rosemary was The Giver's daughter. Selected ten years earlier to become the new Receiver of Memory, she began training with The Giver, but after only five weeks, she asked to be released from the community.

CRITICAL COMMENTARIES

CHAPTERS 1 & 2

In the first sentence of *The Giver*, Lowry creates suspense and foreshadows the outcome of the novel. The setting is an unknown future year in "almost December." Lowry uses the word *December* to symbolize short, dark days, cold weather, and endings—a time when nature seems dead. She also alludes to future, fearful situations because Jonas' fear—apprehension—has just begun. Lowry uses the third person, limited omniscient viewpoint—that is, she tells us what Jonas thinks and feels but not what the other characters' thoughts and feelings are. This viewpoint is limited omniscient because the thoughts and feelings of only one character, the protagonist, are revealed.

Although Lowry doesn't provide geographical details of Jonas' community, she does disclose certain characteristics of the community through Jonas' point of view. As Jonas remembers an incident a year earlier when a pilot mistakenly flew over the community, it becomes evident that the people in the community unhesitatingly obey instructions that the Speaker blasts over loudspeakers placed throughout the community. At the conclusion of the plane incident, the Speaker uses an amused tone to announce that the pilot is going to be "released" from the community. Through Jonas, we know that a release is a "terrible punishment, an overwhelming statement of failure." The irony of the Speaker's amused tone and the pilot's serious punishment creates a sense of foreboding—a threatening feeling that something bad is going to happen—because Lowry does not explain what "release" means.

Jonas' life seems ideal. His parents both work. His father is a Nurturer, a caretaker of infants, and his mother has an important job with the Department of Justice. Jonas and his seven-year-old sister, Lily, attend school, and Lily goes to the Childcare Center after school. Jonas and Lily argue and tease each other. Each evening at mealtime, the family members share their feelings about that day's events and then comfort and support each other. Their life seems too good to be true.

Not only Jonas' family but the entire community appears to be a utopia, a perfect place where nothing bad happens. Everyone who is at least nine years old rides bicycles because they seem to be conscious of improving their air quality by not using vehicles. Children eight years old and younger are not allowed to ride bicycles until they receive their own at the age of nine, but, like most children, they secretly practice. The elderly people in the community are honored for a life well lived and are released at celebrations of their lives. Each school day begins with a patriotic hymn—a "chanting of the morning anthem"—and citizens of the community encourage the use of precise language.

Precise language, however, is not always precise. Many times, the meaning of a word is other than the dictionary meaning. For example, during the evening sharing of feelings, Lily explains her anger at a boy who visited her school that day but who didn't understand the playground rules. The visitor behaved differently, so Lily and Jonas call him an "animal." To them, the word "animal" means "someone uneducated or clumsy, someone who didn't fit in." However, Lily and Jonas don't really know what an animal is because apparently animals do not exist in their community. That people in the community, because they have never had contact with animals, believe that animals are imaginary can be seen in the comfort objects which Sevens and younger sleep with. Comfort objects are stuffed animals that represent actual animals. Each newchild (infant) is issued one comfort object and can keep it until the age of eight, when it is turned in to be recycled for use by another newborn. Jonas' comfort object was a bear, and Lily's is an elephant.

As Lowry discloses other meaningful details about the community, tension builds because something doesn't seem quite right. We find out that everyone in the community lives by rules contained in the Book of Rules. Adults do not choose their own spouses; instead, they are matched according to their personalities. Each family is called a family unit and is made up of a mother, a father, and two children—one male child and one female child. Parents in a family unit must apply for each child. When their application is accepted and they have been matched with one of the babies born during the year (only a maximum of fifty babies are born each year to control the population), they receive a newchild at the December Ceremony, when the infant is named and becomes a One (one year old). Birthdays are not exact: A child's age always increases each December, even if the child's birthday is not in December. After a person reaches the age of twelve, birthdays are no longer observed.

The community members have chosen Sameness over individuality and security over freedom, both major themes in the novel. Until the age of twelve, each peer group is called by its age—for example, Fives, Sevens, Elevens—and must abide by established rules regarding appropriate clothing, haircuts, and behavior for each particular age group. Every child in a peer group looks the same. Everyone and everything are predictable day after day, year after year, thereby ensuring the false sense of security that people in the community have chosen over the freedoms to think and act for themselves. Jonas' community is not a utopia; it's a dystopia, a place that *appears* to be perfect but really is not.

Lowry gives us the illusion that the people living in the community are acting as individuals rather than as robots. For example, when Jonas' father breaks a rule by checking a list to see what name an infant, who is not sleeping soundly or developing as quickly as he should, will be given at the naming ceremony, Jonas is awed. He can't imagine his father breaking a rule, especially because fathers are expected to exhibit model behavior for their children, and if citizens are caught breaking the rules, they are punished. If someone breaks the rules and is caught three times, the offender's punishment on the third offense is release from the community.

Jonas' mother's duties include punishing people who break rules and ultimately having to authorize these people's release from the community. Her distressful feelings about release show that a release is actually quite horrible. A release is final and signifies that the person being released is a complete failure to the community. Lowry hints at the meaning of release when she describes the citizens' feeling of "what-could-we-have-done?" when an infant has to be released for not developing quickly enough. The people clearly feel as though they are doing the right thing by following the rules, but by following the rules, they don't have to accept responsibility for their actions. They are so conditioned to following the rules that it doesn't occur to them to think as individuals and voice their own opinions. And getting a rule changed is an almost impossible feat. Citizens laugh about changing a rule because it is such a difficult, drawn-out procedure. The suggested rule is first presented to the Committee of Elders and is then studied for years. If the Committee of Elders can't make a decision, the proposed rule change goes to The Receiver, the most important Elder in the community, for a decision. Because the process could take a life-time, changes in the rules are not often suggested.

When Jonas shares his apprehension about the December Ceremony with his parents during the ritualistic evening sharing of feelings, a family discussion ensues. The December Ceremony is especially important to Jonas because he is an Eleven and will be participating in the Ceremony of Twelve, in which he will be as-signed his lifelong career. The job Assignments are secretly made by the Committee of Elders after much observation, note-taking, and discussion. Jonas is apprehensive because he has no idea what his Assignment will be. According to the rules, Jonas' parents com-fort him, assuring him that his Assignment will be the right one for him. At the conclusion of Chapter 2, Lowry continues the book's foreboding mood of uncertainty as Jonas' mother talks to him about the changes that will occur in his life after he is assigned.

(Here and in the following chapters, difficult words and phrases are explained.)

- **dwelling** a home.

- **Food Delivery people** People in Jonas' community don't cook their own food. The food for each meal is delivered to community members by people who have been assigned to be Food Delivery people.

- **ironic** a contrast between what is expected and what actually occurs. For example, in Chapter 1, when the Speaker informs the community that the errant pilot will be released, he uses an "amusing" tone in his voice, but the act of release is a serious, fatal matter.

- **Speaker** the person whose voice the people hear over the loudspeaker system.

- **palpable** here, meaning real.

- **hatchery** Jonas' community includes a salmon hatchery, a place where salmon are raised for the people's consumption.

- **tunic** a piece of clothing.

- **wheedle** here, meaning to compete for attention.

- **animals**   a term used in Jonas' community to describe someone "uneducated or clumsy, or someone who didn't fit in."

- **usages**   ways in which words are used.

- **newchildren**   newborns; infants.

- **supplementary**   additional.

- **December Ceremony**   the ceremony during which the children in each peer group chronologically move from one age to the next; infants are placed with family units, and Twelves are assigned their lifelong careers.

- **Hall of Open Records**   a building that stores records about citizens and events, as well as other information that is available to citizens of the community.

- **comfort object**   a stuffed animal that is issued to an infant until the child becomes an Eight, at which time the stuffed animal is recycled for another child's use.

CHAPTERS 3–5

Two major themes—freedom versus security and individuality versus conformity—are emphasized in these three chapters. Because Jonas' father is concerned about one of the newborns, he requests and receives permission to take the infant, named Gabriel (Gabe), home with him each night for extra nurturing. When Jonas, his mother, and Lily meet Gabe for the first time, Lily immediately comments that Gabe's eyes are like Jonas': different. Both Gabe and Jonas have light, pale eyes. Jonas is upset with Lily for drawing attention to the fact that his eyes are unlike most everyone else's dark eyes. Because people in the community chose Sameness, it is extremely rude to talk about things that are different. Although Jonas is not often reminded of his unique eyes because mirrors are uncommon possessions in the community, Jonas knows that his light eyes are unusual. Lowry foreshadows future events by describing Jonas' eyes and Gabe's eyes as "pale, solemn, knowing eyes" that have depth, suggesting that both Jonas and Gabe may see things that other people can't see.

Gabe's presence prompts Jonas' family's conversation about Birthmothers because Lily hopes that she will be assigned to be a Birthmother when she becomes a Twelve. During the conversation, we learn that Birthmothers give birth to three babies over a three-year period. Each newchild is immediately taken away from its Birthmother and is cared for by Nurturers in the Nurturing Center until the newchild is placed with a family unit at the December Ceremony. Birthmothers become Laborers at the end of their three years of birthing. Jonas' mother tells Lily that there is little honor in an Assignment as a Birthmother, implying that a caste system—a division within a society according to people's professions—exists within the community. Although Jonas' community *appears* to be perfect, prejudices do exist in one form or another.

The people in the community are controlled by announcements and chastisements that are heard over loudspeakers. Apparently, secrets do not exist within the community. Loudspeakers are everywhere, even in the family dwellings. Jonas was once publicly chastised because he took an apple home from the Recreation Area. The Speaker didn't mention Jonas' name over the loudspeaker, but both Jonas and his parents knew that the reprimand was directed at him. He broke a rule, and the next day he promptly apologized to the Recreation Director. Confused and unable to find the precise words to describe what happened to him, Jonas never told anyone why he took the apple. He was playing catch with his best friend, Asher, using the apple as a ball, when suddenly he saw the apple change—Lowry doesn't describe how it changed. Knowing that this strange occurrence was "different," he didn't tell anyone about it. Jonas' uneasy feelings and the hints that Lowry has revealed about Jonas' being different from other community members add to the suspense of the book.

Lowry leads us to believe that Jonas' community is a perfect place to live, or a utopia. When children become Eights, they begin their volunteer hours. These children have the freedom to choose where they want to volunteer; however, because the hours are mandatory, it appears that even this freedom is controlled. The purpose of volunteering is to give the Committee of Elders the opportunity to observe each child in different working situations so that the Elders can make appropriate lifelong career Assignments for the children when the children become Twelves.

At the beginning of Chapter 4, Jonas finds his friends, Asher and Fiona, volunteering in the House of the Old, which is like a present-day nursing home. He volunteers there also. In the House of the Old, the community's elderly people live while awaiting their release.

While at the House of the Old, Jonas is instructed to help bathe the Old in the bathing room. We learn that it is against the rules for anyone to look at any naked person except at infants (newchildren) and the Old. While bathing a woman named Larissa, Jonas thinks that the bathing room feels safe because Larissa looks trusting and free. These feelings are ironic because people gave up their freedoms when they decided to live in a community of Sameness. Their feeling of security is an illusion, a false appearance.

Larissa speaks to Jonas about the release of an Old named Roberto. At the release ceremony, which was held earlier that morning, Roberto's life story was told before he was released. According to Larissa, the ceremony is designed to make each person's life sound meaningful. Larissa corrects herself to say that all lives *are* meaningful. Here, Lowry uses irony once again to emphasize a key theme: The people are under the impression that their lives are meaningful, but in reality they all live meaningless lives. They behave like robots because they chose Sameness over individuality (differences). Larissa also mentions that she doesn't think a woman named Edna, who has been released, was "very smart." Larissa's comment about Edna shows that people in the community *do* judge one another and are aware of differences despite their efforts to create a community of uniformity. Control of the people is once again emphasized when Larissa and Jonas suggest changing a rule and then laugh because it could take a lifetime or longer to get a rule changed.

At the beginning of Chapter 5, during the morning ritual of telling dreams, Jonas tells his family members about his dream during the previous night. He dreamed about wanting to bathe his friend Fiona. He had pleasant feelings during the dream. As a result of Jonas' discussing his dream, his mother tells him that he will have to start taking a pill. She explains that all of the adults in the community take a pill every day to stifle the Stirrings—sexual desires. The pill is another way that the Committee of Elders controls people. Physical affection within the family unit is uncommon, and physical affection or touching outside of the family unit is absolutely inappropriate and rude. Jonas knows that Asher has been taking a pill but never asks him about it because it is rude to talk about such personal things. Jonas takes his pill, feeling proud and sad at the same time—proud because he is doing what all adults do, and sad because within a short time, the pleasurable feelings disappear and he feels the same as before.

- **chastise**   criticize.
- **port**   here, a place to secure a bicycle.
- **Birthmother**   a female who is assigned to give birth to three children within three years, after which she becomes a Laborer.
- **House of the Old**   a facility, similar to a nursing home, in which elderly people reside and are cared for by Caretakers.
- **droning on**   speaking continuously; chattering idly.
- **hoarded**   selfishly accumulated.
- **Caretaker**   a person who cares for the elderly in the House of the Old.
- **Collection Crew**   people assigned to pick up food trays left outside of dwellings.
- **Stirrings**   feelings of sexual desire.

CHAPTERS 6–8

As Chapter 6 begins, Jonas' family unit is preparing to go to the December Ceremony, which lasts for two days. By describing the rules that each peer group must follow, Lowry emphasizes the theme of individuality versus conformity. We learn that Fours, Fives, and Sixes are required to wear jackets that button up the back. With buttons on the back, the children are forced to help each other button and unbutton the jackets and thus will learn interdependence. Sevens receive front-button jackets, symbols of independence. Girls must wear hair ribbons until they become Nines, and Eights begin volunteering and wearing jackets with smaller buttons and pockets. The pockets symbolize the responsibility and maturity of all Eights. Tens get their hair cut; male Elevens receive longer pants, and female Elevens receive new underwear because their bodies are physically changing.

Just when we begin to doubt that this community is really such a good place to live in after all, Lowry interjects normalcy. Lily "fidgets" as her mother braids her hair, Jonas and Lily joke and tease each other, and their mother wants to leave early to get a good seat in the Auditorium for the Ceremony. This scene is not unlike a scene in any family.

The theme of individuality versus conformity is especially important as Lowry relates Gabe's status. Rather than be labeled "Inadequate" and immediately be released from the community because he hasn't gained the weight required of babies his age and doesn't yet sleep through the entire night, Gabe has been given a reprieve, a second chance. Thanks to Jonas' father, he has been labeled "Uncertain" and has a year in which to improve. Gabe is different from others his age, which is unacceptable to the community, but he is fortunate: He is able to spend each night with Jonas' family unit and receive extra attention and care. The only stipulation, or condition, to this arrangement is that Jonas' family members must sign a pledge stating that they will not become emotionally attached to Gabe. They can care for him physically, but they are not allowed to love him. The only way to maintain the illusion of social order within the community is to enforce the rules and make sure that everyone conforms. Individual feelings interfere with established rules.

Everyone in the community attends the December Ceremony, which is held in the Auditorium. The Ceremony begins with the Naming and Placement of newborns. When Jonas' friend Fiona goes onstage with her parents, they are given a male infant named Bruno. The previous year, the family unit of Jonas' friend Asher was given a female newchild named Phillipa. Asher is eleven years older than Phillipa, and it is unusual to have such a large age gap between two children in the same family unit. Only four years separate Jonas and his sister, Lily. On this occasion, one family receives a "replacement child," named Caleb, because their first child, also named Caleb, wandered off and fell into the river that runs near the community. For a family unit to lose one of its two children is a rare occurrence in the community. When everyone follows the rules and acts the same (conforms), nothing bad happens, and the community remains an extremely safe place to live. When people don't follow the rules, they are considered inferior because they "infringed on the community's sense of order and success."

During the December Ceremony's Naming and Placement of newborns, we find out that names are "recycled." When an elderly person is released from the community, apparently the released person's name is put on a list and is used again. For example, because an elderly man named Roberto was released in Chapter 4, a newborn is named Roberto and given to a family unit in Chapter 6.

The Ceremony proceeds with each age group in consecutive order. When the Nines receive their very own bicycles, Fritz, who lives in the dwelling next door to Jonas', almost bumps into the podium. Fritz is quite clumsy and is always getting into trouble for such things as not studying for school quizzes, losing his homework, or wearing his shoes on the wrong feet. Fritz's behavior is a problem for his parents because it indicates that they are not good parents; remember, people who do not behave the same as others in the community jeopardize the order and success of the entire community.

When the Ceremony of Twelve begins, Jonas, also known as Nineteen (the number given him at birth because he was the nineteenth child born that particular year), is sitting in the Auditorium in numerical order with the other Elevens. He is comforted with the realization that whatever Assignment he receives will be the right one for him. Rarely are people dissatisfied with their Assignments. If people are unhappy with their Assignments, or if they feel as though they no longer fit in the community, they can apply for release. Again Lowry wants us to question anything that has to do with a release when she has Asher comment, "Here today and gone tomorrow. Never seen again." Applying for release because a person dislikes an Assignment is almost unheard of because the decisions made by the Committee of Elders are meticulously thought out.

The Chief Elder's speech that begins the December Ceremony is ironic because in a community that chooses Sameness and security over individuality and freedom, here the Chief Elder acknowledges the *differences* that have been observed in each Eleven. She says to the Elevens, "You Elevens have spent all your years till now learning to fit in, to standardize your behavior, to curb any impulse that might set you apart from the group." However, although the Chief Elder states that differences exist among the community members, we wonder just how many differences there possibly could be in a community that blindly accepts Sameness.

Asher, Jonas' best friend, is called to the stage for his Assignment. The Chief Elder discusses Asher's difficulty learning precise language. As a Three, Asher would ask for a "smack" rather than a "snack." Each time Asher made this error, the Childcare worker whose responsibility it is to teach the children the importance of precision of language swatted Asher with a discipline wand. For a time, Asher stopped talking. Everyone in the Auditorium laughs at this memory. In our society, this form of "teaching" would be unacceptable. Jonas' community, however, obviously makes it quite clear to the children at a very young age that they must conform and obey—or else. In the midst of what appears to be a celebration and holiday for the community members, Lowry doesn't let us forget the sacrifices that people make when they choose to give up their individuality and freedom.

As the December Ceremony progresses and the Elevens receive their Assignments, the Chief Elder skips over Jonas' name. At first, Jonas thinks that the Chief Elder has made a mistake, but he quickly corrects his thinking because the Chief Elder would *never* make a mistake. Unfortunately, Jonas feels as though he has unknowingly done something wrong and is being punished. In describing the situation, Lowry writes that Jonas "tried to make himself smaller in his seat. He wanted to disappear, to fade away, not to exist." Jonas' feelings of humiliation and terror because he has been skipped over, as well as the confusion that everyone in the Auditorium feels, create suspense in the book. Lowry makes it obvious that Jonas is different, which in Jonas' community is *not* a positive attribute.

After all of the other Elevens except Jonas have been assigned, the Chief Elder apologizes for causing everyone, and especially Jonas, such discomfort by skipping over Jonas' name. Jonas now goes onstage, and the Chief Elder announces that Jonas has not been assigned but, rather, has been "selected" to become the new Receiver of Memory, the most honored position in the community. She explains that as a new Receiver trains, he is to be "alone, apart," so the person selected must be perfect for the position because he can't be observed—except by the current Receiver of Memory, who will train Jonas. During the selection process, if anyone on the Committee of Elders would have had "dreams of uncertainty," the candidate would no longer have been considered for the position of Receiver. When considering Jonas, there were no such "dreams of uncertainty."

The Chief Elder goes on to explain the qualities that a Receiver of Memory must possess. These qualities include intelligence, integrity, courage, wisdom, and the Capacity to See Beyond. Jonas is unsure whether or not he has this last quality, but as he looks out at the audience, he sees the audience change, the same way that the apple changed. Remember that earlier in the book, when Jonas first saw Gabe's pale eyes, which are exactly like his own, Jonas thought that such light eyes had a "certain look . . . as if one were looking into the clear water of the river, down to the bottom, where things might lurk which hadn't been discovered yet." Maybe Jonas does have the Capacity to See Beyond.

Chapter 8 ends with Jonas confused about his future as the new Receiver of Memory. He feels fear because he will have to endure physical pain and will be alienated from his friends and family, but he feels pride because the members of the community are in awe of him—and he hasn't done anything yet. He has only been selected.

- **indulgently** here, meaning patiently, contentedly, and happily.

- **Elsewhere** a place outside of the community; Lowry only hints at what and where Elsewhere is.

- **Ceremony of Loss** When a child dies unexpectedly, the citizens of the community repeat the dead person's name over and over—and more and more softly—during the day.

- **Murmur-of-Replacement Ceremony** When a new infant is given to a family unit to replace a child who died unexpectedly, the citizens of the community speak the child's name softly at first, then more rapidly and loudly, symbolizing the return of the dead child. The new infant is given the same name as that of the child who died.

- **buoyancy** the ability to stay afloat.

- **aptitude** skill or ability.

- **sheepish**   embarrassed and uncomfortable.

- **retroactive**   putting something in effect at an earlier time.

- **ruefully**   regretfully or sadly.

- **piecemeal**   scattered; not together or in unison.

- **benign**   not harmful; gentle and calm.

- **indolence**   laziness.

- **Capacity to See Beyond**   having the ability to see things that others cannot see.

CHAPTERS 9 & 10

In Chapter 9, Jonas realizes that his life will never be the same as a result of having been selected as the new Receiver of Memory. At the conclusion of the December Ceremony, Jonas immediately feels "separate, different." People move aside for him to pass, and his peers are unsure of how to act toward him. Even his best friend, Asher, appears uncomfortable in Jonas' presence. His peers' reactions cause Jonas to feel very much alone and isolated. For the first time in his life, Jonas does not feel the same as everyone else. Lowry describes Jonas' demeanor as uneasy, nervous, and worried, suggesting that he is quite unhappy.

Jonas questions his parents about the last person who was selected to be the Receiver of Memory. They tell him that the person was a female, but they don't know what happened to her, only that her name is "Not-to-Be-Spoken." Jonas knows that something terrible happened to the girl because a "Not-to-Be-Spoken" name means total humiliation and dishonor. Jonas' parents become silent, making no further comments about the previously selected Receiver. Jonas now seems isolated even from his family.

The only similarity between Jonas' Selection and everyone else's Assignment is the folder of instructions that each Twelve receives for his or her lifelong career. Lowry uses rhetorical questions—questions to which oftentimes there are no answers—to portray Jonas' feelings of disbelief after he reads his list of instructions. For example, Jonas wonders, "What would happen to his friendships? His mindless hours playing ball, or riding his bike along the river?" He has no choice but to do what is expected of him, but he feels that his childhood is slipping away.

Jonas' instructions do not allow any time for recreational activities, and what is most shocking to Jonas is that some of the instructions directly contradict the rules that he has followed throughout his life. Because behavior in his community is based on respect and politeness, he has never dared to ask questions or be rude, but his instructions indicate that now he can. He is *not* to discuss his dreams or accept medication for pain that has to do with his training. Jonas feels scared when he thinks about the "indescribable" pain that will be inflicted upon him during his training. However, he doesn't really know what pain is, for pain is "beyond his comprehension." And he can lie. Jonas has never intentionally lied. He recalls an incident when he used the word "starving" rather than "hungry." Accused of lying, he was told that no one in the community was, or ever would be, starving. Precision of language prohibits any lying and controls inappropriate thoughts. For the first time, Jonas is faced with the possibility that his entire community could be based on a lie, and every single person could be lying. And if people are lying, then the community itself and its utopian ideals are also lies.

Along with the obvious changes in Jonas' life, such as the nameplate that is changed on his bicycle by the Maintenance Crew during the night, Lowry reveals details about the current Receiver's accommodations, called the Annex, that indicate that Jonas' life has dramatically changed and will never be the same. Jonas is surprised to find that the doors at the Annex can be locked. He is unaware of any other doors in the community that lock. Also, The Receiver's furniture is different: It has curved lines and is decorative. In all other dwellings in the community, the furniture is the same: functional. The fabrics on the current Receiver's chairs and bed are luxurious, and, to Jonas' amazement, the walls are lined from top to bottom with shelves holding thousands of books. He hadn't known that so many books existed. The only books he knew about were his school books, the training manuals, reference books, and, of course, the Book of Rules. By limiting the citizens' access to books, the Committee of Elders is able to exert control over the community. Allowing people to be exposed to different ideas, places, or characters found in books jeopardizes Sameness; books represent knowledge, which in turn represents individual freedom to make choices in life.

Jonas meets the current Receiver of Memory and notices that The Receiver's eyes are pale like his own (and like Gabe's, although Jonas doesn't think of this similarity). When The Receiver tells Jonas that The Receiver's job is to transmit all the memories of the world to Jonas, Jonas doesn't understand because concepts having to do with "world" and "memories" are unknown to him. He knows "only us, only now." Here, Lowry introduces a major theme in the novel: the awareness that people must have about the interdependence between human beings, the environment, and the world. The current Receiver explains to Jonas how the future is developed based on wisdom gained from memories of the past.

The Receiver tells Jonas that the numerous apologies that are expected in the community and the rote acceptance-of-apology response are unnecessary between them. Lowry demonstrates how language is used to control the people by pointing out that the numerous apologies and trained response are *automatic* for the citizens in the community. The politeness that people exhibit toward each other is an illusion of social order. Although people appear to be considerate of each other, they really aren't sorry for their actions because their responses have been *trained*. Blindly obedient, they apologize and accept apologies without thinking because they are following the rules. Here, Lowry emphasizes an important theme regarding the importance of maintaining individuality: When people stop thinking for themselves and blindly follow a group, bad things can—and usually do—happen.

Lowry concludes Chapter 10 with a mood of suspense as the current Receiver turns off the loudspeaker, which, as another means of controlling people, cannot be turned off in family dwellings. He tells Jonas to take off his tunic and to lie face down on the bed. Jonas is about to receive his first memory.

- **solemnly**   seriously, with awe.

- **exempted**   freed; not responsible.

- **relief-of-pain medication**   medication that is dispensed to community members to relieve pain so that no one in the community suffers.

- **integral** necessary.

- **alcove** a small area set off from a larger room or space.

- **conspicuous** noticeable.

- **embossed** Embossing is a process in which letters or shapes are physically raised—for example, words in books printed in Braille; if you run your finger over the embossed letters or shapes, you can feel their outline.

- **runners** blades used to glide over a surface, usually ice.

CHAPTERS 11 & 12

As the current Receiver of Memory transmits the first memory to Jonas, Lowry's style of writing changes. Up to this point, her style has been straightforward—clear and uncomplicated. However, all of the memories, which we understand through Jonas' interpretations of them, are lyrical because Jonas' thoughts, feelings, and moods are portrayed, as are the vivid images of what he experiences. For example, to describe Jonas' ride on the sled, Lowry gives us sensory impressions by using lyrical phrases such as "the sharp intake of frigid air" and "cold swirling around his entire body"; snowflakes are "tiny, cold, featherlike feelings," Jonas holds a "rough, damp rope," and the snowstorm looks like a "bright, whirling torrent of crystals." Because Jonas has never experienced snow, his sensations are unexplainable, but he feels a sense of peace at the conclusion of receiving the memory.

After Jonas receives the memory of the sled ride, he asks about the snow and the hills. The current Receiver, who later tells Jonas to call him The Giver, explains that generations ago, when the people chose Sameness, they also chose Climate Control and a flat terrain because the community could produce more food, and transportation would be easier and faster without hills, curves, and hazardous weather. The people believed that Sameness would benefit the community. Jonas expresses his wish that he and everyone else in the community had the option to choose. But, as The Giver reminds him, the people *did* choose: They chose Sameness. Lowry once again returns to a key theme in the novel. When people choose Sameness and security, they give up their individuality and

OUACHITA TECHNICAL COLLEGE

the freedom to make further choices. Instead, all further choices are made *for* them.

The Giver transmits two more memories to Jonas that are as lyrical as the first memory. Jonas receives a memory of sunshine that is as pleasurable as the sled-riding memory. Confused, Jonas questions The Giver about the pain that he'd been told he would have to endure. Suggesting the pain that Jonas will feel in memories that he has yet to experience, The Giver sighs and hesitates answering Jonas' questions, as though he is not sure how to tell Jonas about the pain that is to come. To help explain the pain that awaits Jonas, The Giver transmits the memory of a painful sunburn to Jonas. Afterward, Jonas comments that he now understands pain. The Giver does not respond, indicating that Jonas doesn't know pain at all. Here, Lowry creates suspense because we have been told that Jonas will have to endure *indescribable* pain.

Chapter 12 begins with Jonas eating his morning meal. He had a dream the previous night, but according to his training instructions, he doesn't tell his family about it. In the dream, Jonas is going downhill on a sled in the snow toward a certain destination, but he can't reach the destination. He knows only that the destination welcomes him and is important: "Always, in the dream, it seemed as if there were a destination: a *something*—he could not grasp what—that lay beyond the place where the thickness of snow brought the sled to a stop." Jonas' dream foreshadows the ambiguous end of the book, when Jonas and Gabe are poised finally to reach the place that Jonas cannot yet grasp here in his dream. He has a good feeling after the dream, but he can't figure out why he has this emotion, nor can he forget the feeling as he prepares for school.

At school, Jonas feels alienated from his friends because he can't discuss his training in the same way that everyone else does. By using rhetorical questions, as she did in Chapter 9, Lowry reveals Jonas' thoughts about how absurd it would be for him to try to explain his recent experiences to his peers, who could not possibly understand them because all that his friends know is Sameness. Jonas, however, knows that his life now includes much more than Sameness.

A quality that the Chief Elder believed Jonas possesses is the Capacity to See Beyond. Jonas saw the apple change when he threw it to Asher, and when he was onstage during the Ceremony of Twelve, the faces in the audience changed. One day, Jonas sees Fiona's hair change. When he asks The Giver about all of these experiences, The Giver explains that when the community chose Sameness, the people gave up color, and what Jonas saw was the color red. Because the community wanted to do away with all differences as a way to control the people and their environment, genetic scientists are still trying, as they have for generations, to eliminate any and all colors that exist in people and the environment to attain absolute Sameness. The Giver says, "We gained control of many things. But we had to let go of others." Jonas is angry that the people chose to give up colors and other wonderful experiences in order to attain Sameness. The Giver is surprised at the intensity of Jonas' feelings and the insight that Jonas already has about the philosophy of Sameness.

- **Climate Control** Jonas' community controls the weather so that it is the same all the time.

- **obsolete** of no consequence or importance; forgotten.

- **conveyance** here, meaning transportation.

- **fretful** agitated or uneasy.

- **shed** here, meaning discard or forget.

- **admonition** warning.

- **"seeing beyond"** seeing things that other people in the community can't see because they do not have the memories and no longer have the ability; for example, Jonas sees the color red in Fiona's hair.

- **genetic scientists** here, scientists who study human genes and attempt to eliminate differences, or unique characteristics, in people and in the environment.

CHAPTERS 13–15

Throughout these chapters, Jonas' character grows in complexity as he gains wisdom from the many memories that The Giver transmits to him. Some days, The Giver sends Jonas away because The Giver is in too much pain to be able to train Jonas. Jonas

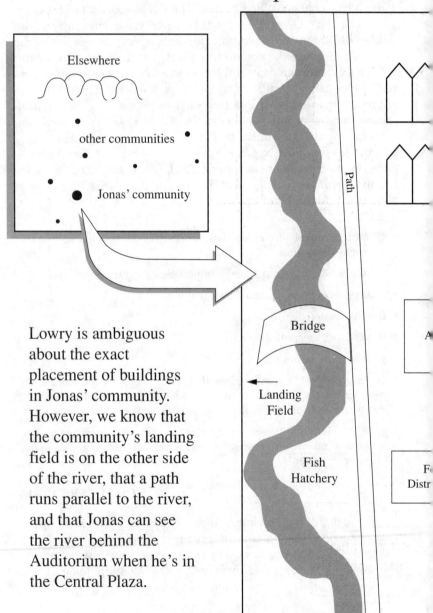

Lowry is ambiguous about the exact placement of buildings in Jonas' community. However, we know that the community's landing field is on the other side of the river, that a path runs parallel to the river, and that Jonas can see the river behind the Auditorium when he's in the Central Plaza.

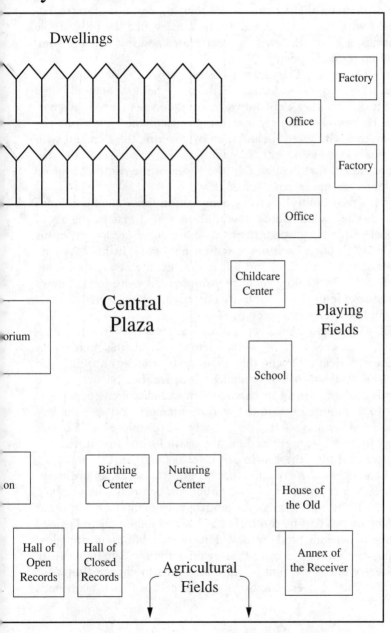

Dwellings

Factory

Office

Factory

Office

Childcare
Center

Central
Plaza

Playing
Fields

orium

School

on

Birthing
Center

Nuturing
Center

House of
the Old

Hall of
Open
Records

Hall of
Closed
Records

Agricultural
Fields

Annex of
the Receiver

spends this free time by himself, disappointed and worried about his future and about The Giver. Because The Giver must unload some of the pain that he carries, he shares memories of excruciating pain with Jonas. These painful memories, like the pleasurable memories, are lyrical. Lowry's descriptions and imagery are similar to that found in poetry.

In Chapter 13, The Giver transmits a painful memory of an elephant hunt to Jonas, during which an elephant is shot and killed for its tusks. Another elephant walks up to the dead elephant's mutilated body and seemingly comforts the elephant by stroking the dead animal with its trunk and then by covering the elephant with branches. Jonas has never before witnessed or experienced the raw emotional pain that is often felt as a result of the death of a loved one; Jonas has never experienced death.

In the next painful memory conveyed in these chapters, Jonas breaks his leg while riding downhill on a sled and learns about physical pain: "He gasped. It was as if a hatchet lay lodged in his leg, slicing through each nerve with a hot blade. In his agony he perceived the word 'fire' and felt flames licking at the torn bone and flesh." After feeling such intense physical pain, Jonas knows that the people in the community don't really know what pain is. They all live overly protected lives.

The Giver now includes pain in Jonas' everyday training, and, finally, Jonas receives the worst memory of all: the memory of warfare and death. During this memory, he watches a "wild-eyed horse, its bridle torn and dangling, [trot] frantically through the mounds of men, tossing its head, whinnying in panic." Jonas gives water to a wounded boy in the warfare memory and sees the boy die, a "dull blankness [sliding] slowly across his eyes. He was silent." Jonas has experienced human death for the first time.

After receiving these memories, Jonas changes. He feels frustrated and angry as he realizes that his life will never be "ordinary" again. He experiences an inner conflict: On one hand, he wants to go back to the old, insulated, familiar way of life; on the other hand, he knows that he can't. He has learned too much and gained too much wisdom, and he now knows that life is meaningless without memories. He can never again settle for Sameness. Also, he is angry and frustrated because he wants to change things for his peers, but he doesn't know how. He realizes that if his friends and family would receive memories and thereby share the burden of the pain, then their lives would be rich and fulfilled. It frustrates him that they are satisfied with their painless, colorless, routine lives.

Jonas also has a conflict with the entire community. The Giver tells him that the people "don't want change. Life here is so orderly, so predictable—so painless. It's what they've chosen." Jonas has a difficult time understanding why people would *choose* to live their lives as unthinking, unfeeling robots, preferring that way of life because it is safe and secure over individuality and the freedom to make choices and, yes, even mistakes.

In small ways, Jonas attempts to change people. After receiving the memory about the elephant hunt, he tries to share his new-found knowledge of elephants with Lily and his father. The idea comes to him one evening when Lily is playing with her comfort object, which is a stuffed elephant, while Jonas' father is combing Lily's hair. Jonas touches each of them on the shoulder, trying to give each of them the *"being"* of a real elephant. However, Lily complains that Jonas is hurting her, and Jonas' father never responds. Disappointed, Jonas removes his hands from their shoulders.

Another illustration of Jonas' trying to break community members of their Sameness occurs when he attempts to show the color red to Asher, who is standing with Jonas near a flowerbed of bright red geraniums. Jonas wants to share color with Asher. Disregarding the rule that it is rude for a person to touch anyone who is not part of the person's family unit, Jonas puts his hands on Asher's shoulders and instructs him to look at the flowers. He tries to "transmit the awareness of red." Asher, feeling quite uncomfortable, moves away, and Jonas, sighing, makes up a story about the flowers wilting and needing water.

Jonas becomes accustomed to asking The Giver questions. Through The Giver's answers, he learns about the kind of life he can look forward to as the Receiver of Memory. He will be able to apply for a spouse and children (The Giver's spouse now lives with other Childless Adults), but his life will be strained. Like The Giver, he will not be allowed to talk about his work, not even to his wife; because books are forbidden to citizens, he will not be allowed to share them with anyone. His life will be difficult because of the burden of pain, and he will be extremely lonely.

Because the Committee of Elders seldom asks The Giver for advice, The Giver spends the majority of his time alone with his memories. The Giver tells Jonas about the two times when the committee asked for his advice. Once, the Elders were considering an increase in population because they wanted to have more Laborers. The Giver advised against it because he had memories of situations involving too many people and not enough food, and the people starved. The committee also sought The Giver's advice the time a pilot mistakenly flew over the community—supposedly the incident that begins this novel. The committee wanted to shoot down the plane immediately, but The Giver advised against such action because his memories include times in which people impulsively shot at planes and ended up bringing about their own demise. The Giver explains to Jonas that gaining knowledge from the memories is what makes the memories invaluable.

Confused, Jonas questions why a Receiver is needed if the Committee of Elders never asks for advice. The Giver explains that the real reason why the Elders value the Receiver of Memory is because The Receiver carries the burden of all pain; without The Receiver, the people would have to share in painful memories. And, of course, the people do not want to feel pain. Ten years earlier, the female who had been selected to be The Receiver failed. When she was released, the memories that she had already received from The Giver were then experienced, or felt, by the people, causing them great discomfort. They were reminded of feelings and memories. The chaotic situation that the people experienced when this new Receiver failed emphasizes the notion that everyone is interdependent, an important theme in the novel.

Jonas feels more and more comfortable talking to The Giver and is surprised when, quite often now, The Giver sounds bitter and cynical about the choice that the people have made to acquire Sameness. The Giver remarks that Jonas' instructors are well-trained, but they have only book knowledge, and book knowledge alone is meaningless without the memories from which wisdom is gained. All of the knowledge in the world is meaningless if a person cannot think freely as an individual.

Over time, Jonas gains insight about life in his community. Lowry again uses rhetorical questions—questions to which oftentimes there are no answers—to reveal Jonas' thoughts as he begins to think for himself. He wonders about hills, about where Elsewhere is located, and about what it might be like to experience Elsewhere. When his father mentions that twins will soon be born and that one of the twins will be released, Jonas wonders if someone will be waiting for the released twin in Elsewhere, who that person will be, and how the twin will grow up. Thinking as an individual, Jonas becomes increasingly frustrated. He is adamant about wanting to change things. He wants the people to have memories, and he wants to share the burden of pain with them. Lowry suggests what the future holds for Jonas and The Giver when The Giver admits that he's "never been able to think of a way" to force the people to accept memories, a statement that indicates that The Giver, like Jonas, wants to do away with Sameness in the community.

Jonas begins to make changes in his own small way. Gabe, the infant who has been spending nights with Jonas' family unit, starts sleeping in Jonas' room at night. The first night that Gabe sleeps in Jonas' room, Gabe wakes up as usual, fussing. To quiet Gabe, Jonas transmits a calming memory to him, something that Jonas was unable to do to Lily and his father. Gabe immediately falls back to sleep. Jonas is frightened of his power. Lowry uses this incident to create suspense. Even though Jonas is afraid, he seems compelled to fight for freedom and individuality, knowing that these qualities are best for the people. Having knowledge and wisdom, Jonas cannot sit idle. He will have to act.

- **geraniums** common house or garden plants that have white, pink, or red flowers.
- **sinuous** curving and supple.
- **assimilated** absorbed.
- **electrode** a conductor through which electric charge is passed.
- **invigorating** powerfully exciting.
- **ominous** threatening.
- **parched** dried.
- **carnage** here, meaning a mutilated and bloody body.

CHAPTERS 16 &17

After receiving the painful warfare memory in Chapter 15, Jonas is reluctant to see The Giver again. The pain that he experienced causes him to mature, and, as a result, he loses his innocence and his childhood. He does return to The Giver, though, because he knows that "the choice was not his."

To help Jonas through the pain that he's experienced, The Giver concentrates on transmitting good, happy memories to Jonas. As in the previous memories, Lowry's style becomes lyrical, and the sense impressions that she creates are extremely realistic. For example, Jonas experiences a birthday party and understands "the joy of being an individual, special and unique and proud." He goes to a museum and sees paintings painted with the many beautiful colors that he now knows exist. He rides a horse across a field that smells of "damp grass" and learns about the bonds that exist between animals and human beings. Also, he spends time learning about the joy and contentment that come from enjoying solitude, or time by oneself.

One day, The Giver transmits his own favorite memory, a memory of love and happiness, to Jonas. In the memory, Jonas is inside a house, and it is snowing outside. A fire is burning in a fireplace, creating a cozy atmosphere, and colored lights decorate a Christmas tree. People are laughing as they open presents and hug each other. They appear to be very happy. From this memory, Jonas learns about a traditional Christmas celebration and about the concept of grandparents. Most important, he learns about love, which, sadly, "was a word or concept new to him."

That night following the Christmas memory, Jonas courageously asks his parents if they love him. They laugh at him and remind him that he needs to use precise language. They tell him that the word *love* is too generalized a word, so meaningless that "it's become almost obsolete." His mother even asks him if he "understands why it is inappropriate to use a word like 'love.'" Dumbfounded by his mother's response, Jonas again faces the realization that his own parents, as well as everyone in the community, stopped having individual feelings when they chose Sameness. His parents don't know what love is. Jonas feels sad because he has experienced love, and love *does* have meaning for him. At the conclusion of Chapter 16, Lowry foreshadows the future when Jonas whispers to Gabe that life in the community could be different if people would change: "There could be love."

Lowry leads us to believe that the mood of Chapter 17 will be less serious than in previous chapters. An unscheduled holiday is announced over the loudspeaker. Everyone has the day off from work, school, training, and volunteer hours. Ironically, Lowry writes, "the community was free." We know, however, that the community is *not* free. The people follow strict rules and can be observed or listened to at any moment by the Committee of Elders. The people chose this way of life because they chose Sameness. Lowry returns, once again, to a significant theme in the novel. When the people chose Sameness, they chose to give up their freedom and individuality, a choice that is ultimately destructive.

Jonas rides his bicycle to find Asher and to enjoy the holiday. While he is riding, he analyzes his feelings, which he now understands have more depth. He compares his own feelings to everyone else's feelings and concludes that people in the community have shallow feelings. Jonas knows from the memories he has newly experienced that the feelings that people discuss during the nightly ritual of emotional sharing cannot simply be discussed; they must be *felt*.

Jonas locates Asher, Fiona, and a group of other children at the playing field. He watches their game, which he has played many times in the past. They are in the middle of an imaginary battle pretending to shoot each other, falling down or running every which way to avoid being shot by the enemy, made up of another group of children. All Jonas can think about while he is watching the make-believe war game is the warfare memory in which the young boy dies. Jonas walks to the middle of the field without thinking about what he is doing and stops the game. The children walk away, uncertain of why Jonas stopped their game of war, and Jonas is left to face Asher and Fiona. He tries to explain how cruel the game is, but, of course, neither Asher nor Fiona understands. They don't understand death either. His friends finally leave.

Jonas' knowledge and wisdom have changed his life. He no longer acts or feels the same way as he did before he began receiving memories from The Giver; therefore, his relationships are not the same. He feels a great sense of loss. Refusing to live as a robot again, he knows that he can never go back to living without feelings (he has even stopped taking his pill for the Stirrings). He feels overwhelming sadness for his friends because they do not feel anything at all.

Lowry leaves us in suspense at the end of Chapter 17 after Jonas finds out that the identical twins will be born the next day and that one of the twins will be released and will go Elsewhere.

• **ecstatic**   exciting and pleasurable.

CHAPTERS 18-20

These three chapters focus on release. Up to this point, Lowry has been vague about the concept of release and has not explicitly stated what release means. She has given the impression that release for older people who are no longer useful to the community, for infants who are different, and for people who are being punished simply means going Elsewhere.

Jonas wonders about release. The Giver explains to Jonas that he himself cannot ask to be released until the new Receiver (Jonas) has been trained. Jonas mentions that his instructions prevent him from asking for release. In a bitter tone, The Giver tells Jonas that the rule about release was added after the Receiver-in-training's failure ten years earlier. At Jonas' request, The Giver finally explains what happened to the earlier Receiver, who was named Rosemary.

Rosemary was selected to be the new Receiver exactly as Jonas was. The Giver began training her, giving her happy, joyful memories until she demanded that he also give her painful and anguished memories. She felt it was her duty to share the burden of pain. But one day, after receiving a few painful memories, Rosemary said goodbye to The Giver, left the Annex, and asked to be released. The Giver never saw her again. As The Giver discusses Rosemary, Lowry provides meaningful details describing The Giver's actions that indicate his overwhelming sadness about Rosemary's decision. While he is talking, he "painfully" hesitates, his voice trails off, and he sorrowfully closes his eyes.

When Rosemary was released after only five weeks of training, the community was in turmoil. All of the memories that Rosemary had received returned to the people in the community. Because memories are forever and are never lost, the people were forced to experience the anguish and the joy contained in the memories. For the first time in their lives, they experienced real feelings. Grief stricken and angry over the loss of Rosemary, The Giver was unable to help the community through its ordeal.

Knowing that memories will destroy the community's Sameness, Jonas asks The Giver a hypothetical question: "What if I fell into the river . . . and was lost?" The answer is clear. Every memory that The Giver has transmitted to Jonas would return to the people, and Sameness would no longer be possible. The community would have to change, and with The Giver's help, the people would endure the experience and benefit from it. Again Lowry foreshadows the future as she concludes Chapter 18 with The Giver deep in thought about Jonas' suggestion to help the community experience freedom once again.

The topic of release is on Jonas' mind because his father was scheduled to release a newborn twin earlier that morning. To Jonas' amazement, The Giver informs Jonas that he can watch the twin's release because all private ceremonies in the community are recorded on video, and being The Receiver, Jonas can ask for anything. Jonas is unaware that the community's every activity is taped. Videotaping everything that goes on in the community is yet another way that the Committee of Elders maintains control of the people.

Concerning the twin's release, Lowry describes in detail the release room in the Nurturing Center. Her style is straightforward, and her tone is foreboding. Suspense builds as The Giver insists in a very firm voice that Jonas be quiet and watch the video recording of the release. Jonas wants to see a release because he thinks that a release is a celebration; he's never had a clue that it is anything else. In an "ordinary room," Jonas' father, talking to the newborn twins, uses the "special voice" that he always uses with newborns. Everything appears to be as it should. Jonas watches as his father sends the heavier newborn twin off to the Nurturing Center and then gives a hypodermic shot into the lighter twin's head. Jonas figures that this shot is a routine vaccination that all newchildren get. He expects that his father is going to make the baby as "comfy" as possible before sending it to Elsewhere. But as Jonas looks at the now-motionless baby, he sees the same blank look on the baby's face that he saw on the dead soldier's face in the memory of warfare. Now Jonas knows that his father has killed the baby. Release means death.

After the video ends, The Giver tells Jonas that Rosemary asked to inject herself at her release. She committed suicide. The anguish that Jonas feels is almost too much for him to bear. He is overwhelmed with betrayal and deceit. When he realizes that his father lies about what releasing a baby means, The Giver sadly explains, "It's what he was told to do, and he knows nothing else." Jonas' community *is* built on lies, which Jonas first suggested at the end of Chapter 9 after he read in his training instructions that he is permitted to lie.

By describing the baby's release, a most senseless and horrifying death, Lowry reveals that the community practices infanticide, the killing of infants. The reason that infants are killed is because they are different in some way. Rosemary's suicide reveals that the community also practices a form of euthanasia—here, meaning that a person voluntarily asks to die. However, in the community, release for the elderly or as punishment for citizens who have br0ken the rules is a form of *forced* euthanasia, or murder.

The emotional climax of the novel is when Jonas finally becomes aware of the true meaning of release and realizes that the community's ideals are far from being idealistic. After watching the release of the smaller twin, everything changes for Jonas and can never be the same again. Jonas refuses to go home. Both angry and sad, he sarcastically mocks people who kill other people in the community. The Giver helps Jonas to understand that the people don't know what they are doing: They are simply following the rules. Because they have no memory of death, loss, pain, and murder, they do not associate a release with any feelings *because they have no feelings*. They gave up their feelings when they chose Sameness. Lowry shows us what can happen when people are blindly obedient to rules. When people give up their freedom to think as individuals, horrible things can—and do—happen. They become robots without the ability to think for themselves.

The falling action of the novel—in literary terms, known as *denouement*—begins as The Giver and Jonas decide that things in the community must change, that neither one of them can tolerate the people's Sameness and blind obedience any longer. Because Jonas and The Giver have the memories, they know that at one time the people in the community also had the memories—before they chose Sameness.

Jonas and The Giver talk until very late, developing a plan to save the people in the community from their own senseless inhumanity. Jonas is willing to risk his life because even if he were to stay in the community, his life would no longer be worth living. Jonas plans to escape to Elsewhere and thereby force the community to share the immense, painful burden of the memories that Jonas has received from The Giver. The Giver will stay in the community to help the people deal with the memories, for if the people don't have The Giver's help, they will probably destroy themselves. Jonas doesn't want to leave The Giver, his only real friend, behind. Although Jonas tells The Giver that they "don't need to *care* about the rest of them," he knows that his statement isn't true. They need to care because caring about others is "the meaning of everything."

Jonas plans to leave the community just before the upcoming December Ceremony. In preparation, The Giver will transmit memories of strength and courage to Jonas. The night before the ceremony, Jonas will leave a note, which his parents will find the next morning, stating that he's gone for an early morning bicycle ride. He will leave his bicycle and some clothing by the river and then go to the Annex. In the morning, The Giver will request a vehicle and driver in order to visit another community. Jonas will hide in the storage compartment of the vehicle. The people in the community will notice Jonas' absence; they will search and assume he's fallen into the river, as the four-year-old Caleb did years earlier. The Giver will then return just in time to perform the Ceremony of Loss for Jonas. The plan seems perfect.

Lowry concludes Chapter 20 by showing the love and affection that Jonas and The Giver have for one another. The Giver tells Jonas that after he helps the people in the community cope with their newly found memories, he wants to be with his daughter, Rosemary, who, we now learn, was the earlier Receiver-in-training who chose death over living a lonely and isolated life filled with painful memories. The Giver is telling Jonas that he is planning to commit suicide.

- **luminous** brightly lit.

- **imploringly** begging for understanding in a painful situation.

- **Hall of Closed Records** a building that houses various documents and video recordings; all information in the Hall of Closed Records is off-limits to the vast majority of citizens.

- **hearing-beyond** hearing things that other people in the community can't hear because they do not have the memories and no longer have the ability; for example, The Giver hears music.

CHAPTERS 21–23

In these last three chapters, Lowry heightens the suspense and tension that have been evident throughout the novel. The plan that Jonas and The Giver have made for Jonas' escape will never be put into action, for on the night after The Giver and Jonas decide on a plan for Jonas to leave the community, Jonas knows that he has to escape immediately. That evening, while Jonas' family unit is eating their evening meal, Jonas' father, using an ironically "sweet, sing-song voice," says, "It's bye-bye to you, Gabe, in the morning." The Nurturers, Jonas' father included, have decided to release (kill) Gabe, but Jonas is not about to let that happen. He cannot allow someone whom he has come to love to be killed for no reason.

The rules of the community no longer matter to Jonas. He chooses to break the rules and save Gabe's life, as well as the lives of the people in the community. Never can he go back to being a complacent citizen in the repressive community in which he's grown up.

Taking Gabe, Jonas leaves his dwelling at night, taking leftover food from the night's supper trays, which have been placed outside doorways for the Collection Crew to pick up. He steals his father's bicycle because he needs the infant seat attached to it for Gabe, who now symbolizes new life and the future.

Jonas does not question his actions. His only regret is leaving The Giver. Because The Giver has the Capacity to Hear Beyond, Jonas calls out a farewell to his friend, hoping that The Giver will hear it. Also, Jonas makes use of his knowledge and abilities by transmitting a calm, peaceful memory to Gabe so that the infant will sleep until they are safely away from the community.

As Jonas and Gabe flee from the community, Jonas' mood changes from anger and frustration to fear and preparation for a fight for survival. Thinking calmly and rationally, he establishes a routine of traveling during the night and then hiding and sleeping during the day. He drinks water from streams, shares the stolen food with Gabe, and transmits calming memories to Gabe so that the infant will sleep. Because Jonas is aware that search planes looking for him are equipped with heat-seeking devices, he also transmits memories of cold and snow to Gabe and uses some of the memories for himself so that their body heat will not expose their location to the search planes.

Days pass, and Jonas and Gabe travel farther and farther away from the community. The memories that Jonas has are becoming dimmer, indicating that these memories are returning to the people in the community. The landscape changes as Jonas and Gabe leave their community of Sameness far behind. They begin to ride during the day because the search for them has subsided. But the journey isn't easy because they are faced with other perils, including forests, streams, and stones that are difficult to ride the bicycle over or through. But they also encounter wonderful things such as birds, various animals, and colorful flowers. Despite the dangers, Jonas has never felt "such simple moments of exquisite happiness."

Although Jonas is able to appreciate the natural surroundings that he encounters on his journey, he is still fearful because he is afraid that he and Gabe will starve to death. The thought crosses his mind that if he'd stayed in the community, he wouldn't be starving from a lack of food. However, he would be starving from a lack of other things that matter in life, including love and freedom. He reaffirms the decision that he made to flee the community. His only sorrow is that he may not be able to save Gabe. Jonas loves Gabe and understands that interdependence between people is necessary and good. He isn't thinking of himself but of Gabe. By saving Gabe, Jonas will be saving himself.

Jonas and Gabe, weakened from a lack of food and living as fugitives, end up in a snowstorm. Luckily, Jonas can recall a memory of sunshine and is able to transmit heat to Gabe, "the one person left for [Jonas] to love." As he did in the dream that he had months earlier, Jonas feels that his destination is not far away, and he feels excited because he knows that he will be welcomed by whomever or whatever awaits him. Carrying Gabe, Jonas trudges up a hill. Finally, they make it to the top. Remembering his parents, sister, and friends, Jonas feels happy despite his situation. At the top of the hill, Jonas finds a sled. He tightly hugs Gabe as they sit on the sled and then begin to go downhill. Jonas sees colored lights in the distance, hears music, and knows that love and joy are at his destination.

In the ambiguous ending of the novel, Lowry blends together Jonas' present situation and his memories so that we don't know if we are reading about a memory or about Jonas' reality. However, because Lowry's style has been lyrical whenever a memory has been transmitted, and because here at the end of the book her style is not lyrical but straightforward, we can assume that Jonas is actually experiencing what we read. Also note that in the second-to-last paragraph in the book's final chapter, Jonas hears—"for the first time"—what he knows is music. Because he never received a memory containing music from The Giver, we can assume that he is not reliving a combination of the sled memory from Chapter 11 and the Christmas memory from Chapter 16. His and Gabe's experience here at the end of the book seems more real than not.

But what happens to Jonas and Gabe? Do they die? Is Jonas really dreaming? Do Jonas and Gabe actually reach a house with colored lights? Are Jonas and Gabe back in their community? Have the people in the community changed because they now have Jonas' memories? Lowry leaves all of these questions unanswered. By concluding the novel so ambiguously, she allows readers the freedom to choose their own endings.

- **languid**   spiritless or weak.
- **augmented**   added to.

- **gullies**   ditches that run parallel to roads.
- **imperceptibly**   without a noticeable result.
- **lethargy**   dullness of spirit; a lack of energy.

CRITICAL ESSAYS

LOWRY'S MAJOR THEMES

Many themes in *The Giver* demonstrate Lowry's concerns about society and humanity. For example, she concentrates on the tradeoffs involved when Jonas' community chooses Sameness rather than valuing individual expression. Certain themes in the book are familiar because they can be found in other novels by Lowry.

Throughout *The Giver*, Lowry attempts to awaken each and every reader to the dangers that exist when people opt for conformity over individuality and for unexamined security over freedom. At one time in the past, the people who inhabited Jonas' community intended to create a perfect society. They thought that by protecting the citizens from making wrong choices (by having no choices), the community would be safe. But the utopian ideals went awry, and people became controlled and manipulated through social conditioning and language. Now, even the expression "love" is an empty ideal. For example, when Jonas asks his parents if they love him, his mother scolds him for using imprecise language. She says that "love" is "a very generalized word, so meaningless that it's become almost obsolete." To Jonas, however, love is a very real feeling.

Lowry stresses the point that people must not be blindly obedient to the rules of society. They must be aware of and must question everything about their lives. In Jonas' community, the people passively accept all rules and customs. They never question the fact that they are killing certain babies simply because such babies are different, or that they are killing old people whom they determine are no longer productive to the community. The community members unquestioningly follow rules; over time, because killing has become a routine practice, horrible and senseless actions do not morally, emotionally, or ethically upset them. As The Giver says of Jonas' father's killing the lighter-weight twin male, "It's what he was told to do, and he knows nothing else."

Another important theme in *The Giver* is the value of the individual. Lowry points out that when people are unable to experience pain, their individuality is devalued. Memories are so vital because they oftentimes include pain, and pain is an individual reaction: What is painful to one person might not be painful to another person. Also, people learn from memories and gain wisdom from remembering past experiences.

Life in Jonas' community is very routine, predictable, and unchanging. So are most of the people who live in the community. These characters are uncomplicated and complacent. They are static, simple, one-dimensional characters. Because the majority of them do not change throughout the novel, we see only one part of their personalities—their surface appearances and actions. Nothing happens *within* static characters; things happen *to* them.

Most of the citizens in the community passively follow the rules of the community. They always do what they are told. Nothing has ever happened to them except when an earlier Receiver-in-training, Rosemary, asked for release because she no longer could tolerate living in the community. After her death, the people were in total chaos because they didn't know what to do with the memories that Rosemary had experienced. They were not accustomed to thinking for themselves. Experiencing Rosemary's memories was something that happened *to* the people. Afterward, they resumed their lives as before, so it is evident that nothing permanently changed within them.

Jonas, on the other hand, is a dynamic character. He changes during the course of the novel due to his experiences and actions. We know how Jonas changes because Lowry narrates *The Giver* in the third person, limited omniscient viewpoint in order to reveal Jonas' thoughts and feelings. When the novel begins, Jonas is as unconcerned as anyone else about how he is living. He has grown up with loudspeakers, rules, precise language, and a family that is not connected biologically, and he has accepted this way of life because he doesn't know any other type of existence. But as he receives The Giver's memories and wisdom, he learns the truth about his community, that it is a hypocrisy and that the people have voluntarily given up their individuality and freedom to live as robots. Jonas' character changes and becomes more complex. He experiences an inner conflict because he misses his old life, his childhood, and his innocence, but he can't return to his former way of life because he has learned too much about joy, color, and love. Lowry writes of Jonas toward the beginning of Chapter 17, "But he knew he couldn't go back to that world of no feelings that he had lived in so long."

Jonas also experiences an external conflict between himself and the community. He is frustrated and angry because he wants his fellow citizens to change and thereby give up Sameness. He knows that the community and each person's life will benefit if only they would—or could—reclaim their individuality. But the people can't change. Generations ago, they chose Sameness over freedom and individuality. Now, they know no other way of life.

Other themes in *The Giver*, such as family and home, friendships, acts of heroism, as well as the value of remembering the past, are familiar because they are themes in Lowry's previous novels also. Like Rabble in *Rabble Starkey*, Jonas has to leave the family that was created for him. Through the experience of leaving, both Jonas and Rabble learn to appreciate what it means to have a family and a home. And like Annemarie in Lowry's award-winning *Number the Stars*, Jonas lives in a repressed society in which he has no freedom. Both Jonas and Annemarie risk their lives in order to save people they love. Because the conclusion of *The Giver* is so ambiguous, we don't know how Jonas' experiences ultimately affect him or his community. We do know that he matures and that he feels excited and joyful as he and Gabe ride down the hill on the sled.

Lowry challenges her readers to reexamine their values and to be aware of the interdependence of all human beings with each other, their environment, and the world in which they live. When people are forced to live under an oppressive regime that controls every person's actions, meaningful relationships between people are threatened because they involve individual feelings and thoughts. Only by questioning the conditions under which we live, as Jonas does in *The Giver*, can we maintain and secure our freedom of expression.

LOWRY'S STYLE AND LANGUAGE

Lowry narrates *The Giver* in a simple, straightforward style that is almost journalistic—one episode directly and logically follows another episode. Her clarity of style and her many everyday details help portray ordinary daily life in Jonas' community. For example, everyone rides bicycles that are neatly stowed in bicycle ports, and families share morning and evening meals and participate in typical family activities. Lowry's descriptions, which are clear and exact, indicate that the community members seem content with their lives. Because everything seems so comfortable and perfect, we are not prepared for the horrible truth that lies hidden beneath this peaceful, utopian surface. Lowry manipulates our perceptions and emotions by slowly and deliberately revealing that Jonas' community is not what it appears to be. Her straightforward style adds to the suspense throughout the novel.

The memories that The Giver transmits to Jonas sharply contrast to Jonas' everyday environment. Lowry describes the memories using a lyrical style. The memories are lyrical—non-journalistic—because they are images that provoke thoughts, feelings, and emotions. The imagery that Lowry creates is similar to that found in poetry. Snow, cold, war, the suffering of animals, and the joy of a celebration or love felt by family members are easily visualized.

Some of the memories that Lowry describes are mystical. They are mysterious because Jonas doesn't fully comprehend them at first. The sensations he feels are unexplainable, but at the conclusion of many of the memories, Jonas feels a sense of peace. This mystical quality is evident in the memory of the family celebrating a traditional Christmas holiday that The Giver transmits to Jonas.

Lowry relies on rhetorical questions—questions to which oftentimes there are no answers—to reveal many of Jonas' thoughts. The unanswered questions that Jonas asks himself show the changes that he is going through as he gains wisdom. These questions emphasize the internal and external conflicts that Jonas experiences. For example, Jonas feels alienated from his friends because he can't discuss his training as the new Receiver in the same way that his peers talk about their job training. Jonas wonders to himself, "How could you describe a sled without describing a hill and snow; and how could you describe a hill and snow to someone who had never felt height or wind or that feathery, magical cold?" By using rhetorical questions, Lowry reveals Jonas' thoughts about how absurd it would be for him to try to explain his recent experiences to his friends, who could not understand them because all that his friends know is Sameness. Jonas, however, knows that life can—and should—include much more than Sameness.

In addition to rhetorical questions, Lowry uses euphemisms to show how easily people's thoughts can be manipulated and controlled without them even realizing it. A euphemism is a term used to say something indirectly or sometimes less offensively. For example, people tend to refer to the elderly as "senior citizens" rather than "old people," or they will say "pass away" instead of "die."

Euphemisms are often used in political situations, usually to cover up or misrepresent an embarrassing incident. Euphemisms are also deceptive. For example, in Jonas' community, the citizens use the word "release" to disguise its real meaning: kill or euthanize. Using euphemisms enables the community members to distance themselves from reality. The word "release" tends to soften the act of violence that is committed.

The community that Lowry creates in *The Giver* stresses precision of language. Precise language, however, in this community, is not precise at all but rather is a language in which the meanings of words are intentionally unclear. For example, each family unit participates in the "telling of feelings" every evening. This sharing is ironic because the people don't have any feelings. They gave up their feelings when they chose Sameness. Another word that is ironic and not precise is "Nurturer." Jonas' father, a Nurturer, is supposed to be a caretaker of infants. He does care for infants, but he also kills them.

One of the reasons why precise language is so very important to the community is that it ensures that nobody ever publicly lies, although at one point Jonas finally realizes that the whole community is a lie. In this way, though, the people can be controlled. As Jonas' mother tells him when he asks her if she loves him, ". . . our community can't function smoothly if people don't use precise language." The use of "precise language" in Jonas' community has contributed to the creation of a non-human society, for the people function as robots and have no feelings. Jonas' parents don't even know the meaning of love. They consider the term meaningless and too general. Even Jonas once comments to The Giver that loving each other is probably a dangerous way to live—even though he likes the feeling.

One important writing technique that Lowry uses in *The Giver* is her open-ended plot structure. To allow readers the freedom to interpret the ending of *The Giver* in their own way, Lowry writes an ambiguous concluding episode to her novel, an ending that is not explained.

After a long journey toward freedom, Jonas and Gabe are freezing and starving. In a horrible, blinding snowstorm, Jonas discovers a sled on top of a hill, just like in a memory that he earlier received from The Giver. Jonas and Gabe get on the sled and begin sliding downhill toward their "final destination." Jonas sees Christmas lights and hears music and singing. He knows that joy, love, and memories lie ahead, but Lowry ends the novel just when we expect her to tell us whether or not Jonas and Gabe reach the town below and what then happens to them.

What happens to Jonas and Gabe? Do they die? Is the sled ride a dream? Do they end up in a different community and find love and joy? Does Jonas' community change? Do Jonas and Gabe end up back in the community that they left? We don't know. The ambiguous ending of *The Giver* has been compared to the ending of Hans Christian Andersen's "The Little Match Girl," in which the main character, a poor little girl, sees Christmas decorations—tinsel and colored balls—and a table laden with food. In Andersen's story, the little match girl freezes to death, but Andersen suggests that she is far happier, for she is "far away where there is neither cold, hunger, or pain." We have to wonder: Could Jonas and Gabe possibly be experiencing a similar kind of euphoria before they, like the little match girl, freeze to death?

Lowry intentionally ends *The Giver* ambiguously to allow each reader to create an individual ending according to that person's own beliefs, hopes, dreams, and experiences. Therefore, every ending is the "right" ending, and every reader, like Jonas, must make a choice. By focusing on Jonas' escape from his community, Lowry portrays how important language, words, freedom of speech, and choice are to the value of the individual, to every society, and to the world in which we live.

WHAT ARE UTOPIAS AND DYSTOPIAS?

The word *utopia* comes from the Greek words *ou*, meaning "no" or "not," and *topos*, meaning "place." Since its original conception, *utopia* has come to mean a place that we can only dream about, a true paradise. *Dystopia*, which is the direct opposite of utopia, is a term used to describe a utopian society in which things have gone wrong. Both utopias and dystopias share characteristics of science fiction and fantasy, and both are usually set in a future in which technology has been used to create perfect living conditions. However, once the setting of a utopian or dystopian novel has been established, the focus of the novel is usually not on the technology itself but rather on the psychology and emotions of the characters who live under such conditions.

Although the word *utopia* was coined in 1516 by Sir Thomas More when he wrote *Utopia*, writers have written about utopias for centuries, including the biblical Garden of Eden in Genesis and Plato's *Republic*, about a perfect state ruled by philosopher-kings. More's *Utopia* protested contemporary English life by describing an ideal political state in a land called Utopia, or Nowhere Land. Other early fictional utopias include various exotic communities in Jonathan Swift's famous *Gulliver's Travels* (1726).

The idea of utopias continued to be popular during the nineteenth century. For example, English author Samuel Butler wrote *Erewhon* (1872) ("nowhere" spelled backward) and *Erewhon Revisited* (1901), and William Morris wrote *News From Nowhere* (1891). In the United States, people have attempted to create real-life utopias. A few of the places where utopian communities were started include Fruitlands, Massachusetts; Harmony, Pennsylvania; Corning, Iowa; Oneida, New York; and Brook Farm, Massachusetts, founded in 1841 by American transcendentalists. Although the founders of these utopian communities had good intentions, none of the communities flourished as their creators had hoped.

Dystopias are a way in which authors share their concerns about society and humanity. They also serve to warn members of a society to pay attention to the society in which they live and to be aware of how things can go from bad to worse without anyone realizing what has happened. Examples of fictional dystopias include Aldous Huxley's *Brave New World* (1932), Ray Bradbury's

Fahrenheit 451 (1953), and George Orwell's *Animal Farm* (1944) and *Nineteen Eighty-Four* (1949).

Lois Lowry chose to write *The Giver* as a dystopian novel because it was the most effective means to communicate her dissatisfaction with the lack of awareness that human beings have about their interdependence with each other, their environment, and their world. She uses the irony of utopian appearances but dystopian realities to provoke her readers to question and value their own freedoms and individual identities.

Jonas' community appears to be a utopia, but, in reality, it is a dystopia. The people seem perfectly content to live in an oligarchy—a government run by a select few—in which a Community of Elders enforces the rules. In Jonas' community, there is no poverty, starvation, unemployment, lack of housing, or prejudice; everything is perfectly planned to eliminate any problems. However, as the novel progresses and Jonas gains insight into what the people have willingly given up—their freedoms and individualities—for the so-called common good of the community, it becomes more and more evident that the community is a bad place in which to live. Readers can relate to the disbelief and horror that Jonas feels when he realizes that his community is a hypocrisy, a society based on false ideals of goodness and conformity. As Jonas comes to understand the importance of memory, freedom, individuality, and even color, he can no longer stand by and watch the people in his community continue to live under such fraudulent pretenses.

A NOTE ABOUT INFANTICIDE AND EUTHANASIA

When Jonas views the release of an infant on The Giver's video screen, he realizes for the first time that "release" means death, or, in this case, infanticide. Release for elderly people or for people who have broken the rules three times also means death, or euthanasia.

Infanticide is the killing of a newborn child. In the past, the main reason for infanticide was due to food shortages among primitive cultures. In most countries today, infanticide is considered a form of murder.

Euthanasia is the method of ending the life of a person who is suffering from incurable pain or disease. Euthanasia can be voluntary, meaning that the person has requested his or her own death, or involuntary, meaning that the person has not explicitly requested death. Euthanasia can also be active or passive. Active euthanasia involves taking deliberate action, such as giving drugs, to cause death. Passive euthanasia takes place when someone is allowed to die by withdrawing life-sustaining treatment.

The ideas of infanticide and euthanasia are not new. In ancient Greece, Plutarch wrote that infanticide was a common practice in Sparta to rid the city of children who "lacked health and vigor." Aristotle, Socrates, and Plato all favored euthanasia but only under certain conditions. As organized religion flourished, euthanasia became morally and ethically condemned by religions such as Christianity, Judaism, and Islam, all of which consider human life to be sacred.

Euthanasia is an extremely controversial subject, and it is easy to imagine how the power to euthanize can get out of hand. In Jonas' community, such power is abused. Anyone who is different, who does not follow the rules, or who is no longer useful to the community is killed. The people in charge, including Nurturers—like Jonas' father—and the Director of the House of the Old, are simply following rules set forth in the Book of Rules, which was established to maintain the safety and security of the community. Like The Giver says about Jonas' father, who kills an infant in Chapter 19, "It's what he was told to do, and he knows nothing else." The irony of killing people who are different in order to maintain Sameness reinforces Lowry's theme that people must be aware of and care about other people.

REVIEW QUESTIONS AND ESSAY TOPICS

1. Analyze the advantages and disadvantages of Sameness in Jonas' community.

2. Compare the relationship Jonas has with The Giver to the relationship he has with his mother, father, and sister.

3. Explain how Jonas' community is hypocritical.

4. Explain why feelings and memories have been eliminated from Jonas' community.

5. Compare *The Giver* to Robert Cormier's *After the First Death* or to Hans Christian Andersen's "The Little Match Girl."

6. Why is Jonas alienated by his friends after being chosen as the next Receiver of Memory?

7. List the ways in which Jonas' community appears to be a utopia and explain why the things on your list contribute to perfection.

8. Discuss whether Jonas' assignment as the next Receiver of Memory is an honor or a punishment.

9. What are some of the euphemisms used in present-day society? Analyze the advantages and disadvantages of using euphemisms.

10. Discuss the value of rules and laws in present-day society.

11. The people in Jonas' community gave up their freedom and individuality to live in a safe environment. Discuss whether or not the community is a safe environment in which to live. How would you define what a safe environment is?

12. What does Jonas take with him on his journey at the end of the book, and why does he take it with him?

13. In the past, and especially in the nineteenth century, utopian communities such as Brook Farm, New Harmony, Oneida, and Shaker settlements were established in the United States. Research one of these communities and then compare it to Jonas' community.

14. How are the people in Jonas' community interdependent?

15. How can Jonas' community be compared to Nazi Germany under Hitler?

SELECTED BIBLIOGRAPHY

LOWRY'S WORKS

Novels

Stay! Keeper's Story. Boston: Houghton, 1997.

See You Around, Sam! Boston: Houghton, 1996.

Anastasia, Absolutely. Boston: Houghton, 1995.

The Giver. Boston: Houghton, 1993; New York: Dell, 1994.

Attaboy, Sam! Boston: Houghton, 1992.

Anastasia at This Address. Boston: Houghton, 1991.

Your Move, J.P.! Boston: Houghton, 1990; New York: Dell, 1991.

Number the Stars. Boston: Houghton, 1989; New York: Dell, 1990.

All About Sam. Boston: Houghton, 1988; New York: Dell, 1989.

Anastasia's Chosen Career. Boston: Houghton, 1987; New York: Dell, 1988.

Rabble Starkey. Boston: Houghton, 1987; New York: Dell, 1988.

Anastasia Has the Answers. Boston: Houghton, 1986; New York: Dell, 1987.

Anastasia on Her Own. Boston: Houghton, 1985; New York: Dell, 1986.

Switcharound. Boston: Houghton, 1985; New York: Dell, 1987.

Anastasia, Ask Your Analyst. Boston: Houghton, 1984; New York: Dell, 1985.

OUACHITA TECHNICAL COLLEGE

Us and Uncle Fraud. Boston: Houghton, 1984; New York: Dell, 1985.

Taking Care of Terrific. Boston: Houghton, 1983; New York: Dell, 1984.

The One Hundredth Thing About Caroline. Boston: Houghton, 1983; New York: Dell, 1985.

Anastasia at Your Service. Boston: Houghton, 1982; New York: Dell, 1984.

Anastasia Again! Boston: Houghton, 1981; New York: Dell, 1982.

Autumn Street. Boston: Houghton, 1980; New York: Dell, 1982.

Anastasia Krupnik. Boston: Houghton, 1979; New York: Bantam, 1981.

Find a Stranger, Say Goodbye. Boston: Houghton, 1978; New York: Pocket, 1979; New York: Dell, 1990.

A Summer to Die. Boston: Houghton, 1977; New York: Bantam, 1979.

Short Stories

"Holding." In *Am I Blue?: Coming Out from the Silence*. Ed. Marion Dane Bauer. New York: Harper Collins, 1994. 177-89.

"Elliot's House." In *The Big Book for Our Planet*. Eds. Ann Durrell, Jean Craighead George, and Katherine Paterson. New York: Dutton, 1993. 116-21.

"The Harringtons' Daughter." In *A Gathering of Flowers: Stories about Being Young in America*. Ed. Joyce Carol Thomas. New York: Harper, 1990. 23-24.

"The Tree House." In *The Big Book for Peace*. Eds. Ann Durrell and Marilyn Sachs. New York: Dutton, 1990. 30-38.

"Splendor." In *Short Takes: A Short Story Collection for Young Readers*. Ed. Elizabeth Segal. Illus. Joseph A. Smith. New York: Lothrop, 1986. 84-105.

"Crow Call." *Redbook* December 1975. 38-39.

CRITICAL WORKS

CAMPBELL, PATTY. "Sand in the Oyster." *The Horn Book Magazine* Nov.-Dec. 1993. 717.

CASTON, JOEL D. *Lois Lowry*. New York: Twayne Publishers, 1997.

Children's Literature Review. Vol. 46. Detroit: Gale Research, 1998. 25+.

Contemporary Authors New Revision Series. Vol. 13. Detroit: Gale Research, 1984. 333-36.

Contemporary Authors New Revision Series. Vol. 43. Detroit: Gale Research, 1994. 280-82.

DINUZZO, TONI, et. al. "Learning About Lois Lowry." *Young Adult Literature*. Online. February 24, 1998.

DONELSON, KENNETH L., and ALLEEN PACE NILSEN. *Literature for Today's Young Adults*. New York: Addison-Wesley Educational Publishers, Inc., 1997.

"Euthanasia." *Microsoft Encarta 97 Encyclopedia*. CD-ROM. Microsoft Corporation: 1993-1996.

FLOWERS, ANN. *"The Giver." The Horn Book Magazine* July-Aug. 1993. 458.

"Infanticide." *Microsoft Encarta 97 Encyclopedia*. CD-ROM. Microsoft Corporation: 1993-1996.

"Lois Lowry." *Internet Public Library.* Online. February 24, 1998.

"Lois Lowry." *Mountain Brook City Schools.* Online. June 2, 1998.

"Lois Lowry." *Bantam, Doubleday, Dell.* Online. June 9, 1998.

LORRAINE, WALTER. "Lois Lowry." *The Horn Book Magazine* July-Aug. 1994: 423.

"Teacher's Guides: *The Giver* by Lois Lowry." *Bantam, Doubleday, Dell.* Online. February 24, 1998.

"Utopias." *Microsoft Encarta 97 Encyclopedia.* CD-ROM. Microsoft Corporation: 1993-1996.

NOTES

NOTES

NOTES

NOTES